BIRD·CARVING
Basics
Volume One

EYES

EYES

Curtis J. Badger

STACKPOLE BOOKS

Published by
STACKPOLE BOOKS
Cameron and Kelker Streets
P.O. Box 1831
Harrisburg, PA 17105

Printed in the United States of America

10 9 8 7 6 5 4 3

First Edition

Cover design by Tracy Patterson

Interior design by Marcia Lee Dobbs

Cover photo: Wood duck carved by Oren Segrest, Jr.
Photographed by Dan Williams, reprinted with
permission from *Wildfowl Carving & Collecting*
magazine.

Library of Congress Cataloging-in-Publication Data

Badger, Curtis J.
   Bird carving basics / by Curtis J. Badger.
     p.   cm.
   Contents: Vol. 1. Eyes.
   ISBN 0-8117-2334-8
   1. Wood-carving. 2. Birds in art. I. Title.
TT199.7.B33 1990
731.4'62—dc20   90-9491
                             CIP

Contents

Acknowledgments

Wildfowl artists are a generous bunch. Instead of harboring private techniques and secret tools, most artists are willing, even eager, to share their knowledge.

There are at least two reasons for this. Bird carvers love what they do and seem to have an almost evangelical zeal to spread the joy. Also, the leading carvers today once sat at the feet of an earlier generation of master carvers, studying their technique and style. And so to them it is only proper to pass along what they have learned.

The carvers represented in this volume are such people. Their work is varied, but all of them were at one time beginners, dependent on someone more fluent to teach them the language of carving. And now, they share their knowledge with you.

Obviously, this book would not have been possible without the generosity of Jim Sprankle, Lee and Leo Osborne, Bob Swain, Pete Peterson, and Grayson Chesser. Before this book was begun, I considered all of them gifted artists, and now I consider them valued friends as well. Many thanks for sharing.

Introduction

In art, there is no right and wrong, only different interpretations of the same vision.

Wildfowl art is a conservative pursuit, bound on one side by tradition and on another by technique. Yet, we don't all see a bird in exactly the same way. We don't experience the same emotion at seeing, for example, a peregrine stooping on a bufflehead, or a robin bringing lunch to her fledglings.

So wildfowl art means much more than simply carving a lifelike bird. Creating the bird is craft. Art is not added until the carver can use craft to share his personal vision, to make his own statement. As in all the arts, bird carving is most successful when it reveals something about the artist as well as the subject.

Carving eyes sounds like pretty pedestrian subject matter. After all, what difference does it make how you do it, as long as the results look good? Adding the eyes to a carving constitutes a very small step in a lengthy carving process, but art is made up of thousands of small steps, each of which you must take on your own. Although this book deals with a very narrow, specific, technical subject, the five examples differ widely in the carvers' motivation, method, and statement. One method is no more correct than any other—except, of course, within the eye and mind of the individual carver who happens to prefer it.

Jim Sprankle's passion is for accuracy, and he's a master at capturing every detail and nuance of a bird. After careers as a professional baseball player and a businessman, Jim became involved in professional carving competitions, and his dozens of blue ribbons attest to his mastery. In competitions, accuracy is essential, and Jim uses every means of achieving this goal. He has an aviary at his studio on Kent Island, Maryland, and he keeps extensive reference files on all the birds he carves.

Bob Swain, on the other hand, believes in suggesting detail rather than stating it outright. His carvings are at once primitive and contemporary, sculptural and decorative. His eyes are carved and painted rather than inserted, and he uses fire as an important tool in the carving and painting process.

For Grayson Chesser, carving is a function of waterfowl hunting. His carvings are meant to be used in a hunting situation; Grayson is happiest when a buyer takes his decoys to the duck blind instead of placing them on the bookshelf. When decoys were first made in America, they were strictly hunting tools, designed for the eye of the bird instead of the eye of man. But when sport hunting became popular around the turn of the century, carvers began making decoys for wealthy sportsmen who wanted the finest shotguns and the finest decoys and were willing to pay well for them. Grayson's carvings seem to go back to an earlier era, when decoys were intended to lure ducks instead of affluent hunters.

Pete Peterson, if he could turn back the clock, would probably set the alarm for two years after the Civil War, and the place would be Cobb Island, Virginia, where Pete would spend his days carving decoys with Nathan Cobb and the boys. Pete's carvings have an element of the hunt in them, but they almost seem like historical artifacts. Pete is a student of the history of the Virginia barrier islands, and he lives in a home that was built by members of the Nathan Cobb family, not far from Cobb Island. Pete's decoys at first glance seem functional, but they also express his passion for this special time and place.

Lee and Leo Osborne are not hunters, nor do they have a passion for realism. Perhaps because of their art school backgrounds and their exposure to a wide array of disciplines, they are difficult to typecast as artists. They have done very realistic carvings and are well known for their wall sculptures of birds on cliff faces, but they also enjoy working in unfinished wood, finding emerging forms in the shapes of the wood itself, such as a peregrine coming out of a redwood burl.

The Osbornes' approach is probably more sculptural than that of the others; they like working with a single block of wood and finding what it has to offer. That's why they like the burning procedure for creating eyes explained in Chapter 2. There are no plastic inserts to dilute the integrity of the wood.

This book presents a wide spectrum of techniques for creating eyes: inserting glass eyes, carving and painting eyes, and burning eyes. There is no single correct method. The best method is the one that works best for you, the one that most fluently expresses your vision of the bird.

1

Jim Sprankle
Inserting the Eyes in a Cinnamon Teal

Jim Sprankle is a perfectionist, which is one of the reasons he's won dozens of awards as a professional wildfowl woodcarver. Another reason is that he is an artist, and he brings to the carving process not only technical virtuosity but also a highly developed sculptural sense.

Jim's carvings are scrupulously realistic. An aviary is attached to his carving studio on Maryland's Eastern Shore, and Jim spends many hours studying and photographing birds before he begins a carving. These sessions help him not only to carve a bird with correct detail and scale, but also to learn the nuances of avian behavior that give his carvings an edge in the competitions.

Jim uses as much reference material as he can muster. In addition to his aviary, he keeps a comprehensive file on every species of bird he carves. This reference material might include photographs, books, study skins, taxidermy specimens, and videotapes. He also uses plastic casts of heads and bills, which show every bump and wrinkle. With such material, Jim is able to produce birds that are remarkably lifelike.

In this session, he locates and inserts the eye in a cinnamon teal. While many carvers locate the eye visually, perhaps drawing and erasing it until it looks proper, Jim has actually taken a measurement from a live cinnamon teal, determining the distance between the corner of the bill and the eye socket. Jim used dividers to transfer this measurement to an index card, which he keeps in his reference file for cinnamon teals. He also uses the cast study bird to double check this measurement.

Jim drills the eye sockets with a conical bit, making the second socket slightly larger than the first so he can move the glass eye slightly, correcting any alignment problems. He uses wood filler as a mounting medium, and while the filler is still wet he uses solvent and a brush to clean it from the eye and to smooth the surface. A final touch of realism is a small bead of plumber's seal, which is placed around the eye to replicate the eye membrane of the waterfowl.

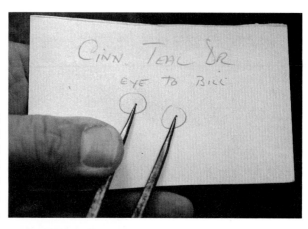

Jim's aviary provides an invaluable reference. He took the eye-to-bill measurement from a live teal and transferred it to this card, which he keeps with other reference material in his "cinnamon teal" file.

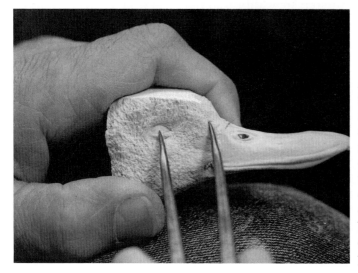

A plastic cast study bird is used to confirm the measurement. Dividers are used to transfer the measurement to the carved wooden head of the teal. "Because our criterion in competitive carving is the lifelike bird, you need all the reference that's available to you," says Jim.

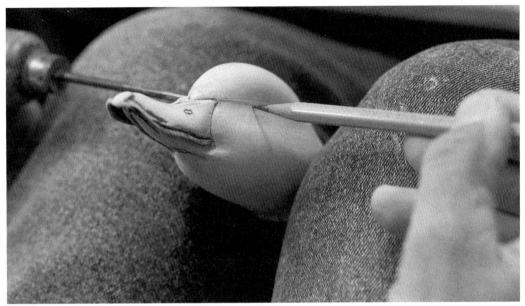

Jim uses an awl and a pencil to line up the two eyes of the cinnamon teal. Two push pins also work well. Jim does not predrill eye holes. Instead, he carves the bill first because the location of the eye is dependent on how the bill is carved.

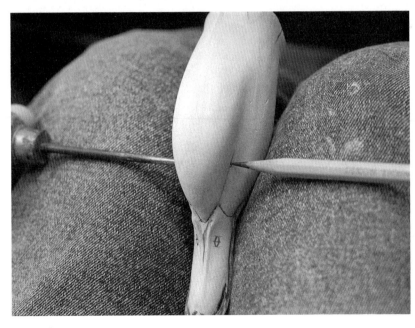

He checks from the front of the bird, and from the top of the head, to make sure that the eyes are aligned. Tools such as these aid your eye in aligning the points.

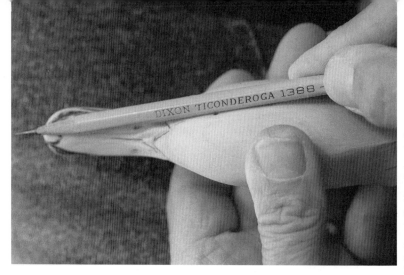

Jim uses a pencil to align the eye socket with the bill. The duck must be able to see the tip of its bill, and this procedure ensures proper alignment.

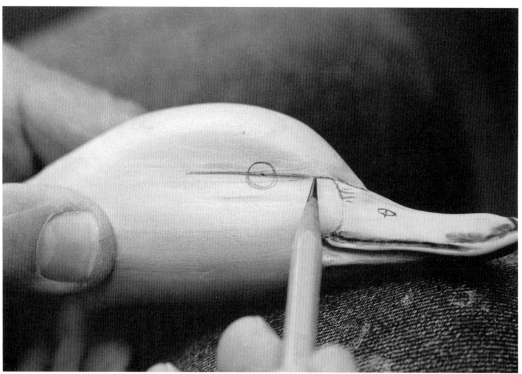

A pencil line shows the alignment of the eye socket location with the bill.

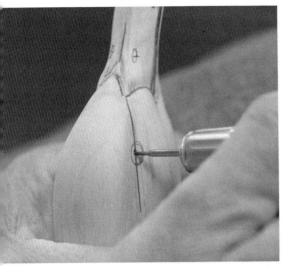

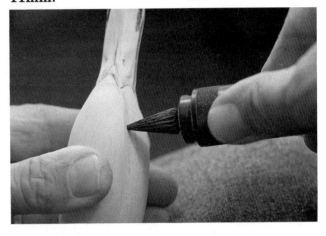

The Foredom tool with a cone-shaped cutter is used to drill the eye hole. The cutter will drill a hole for an eye up to 11mm.

The right eye socket is drilled first. Jim uses a small drill bit to begin a pilot hole, ensuring that the larger bit used to drill the socket will not wander.

Jim uses plastic eyes that do not have wire mounting shafts. As he nears the correct eye socket size, he test fits the plastic eye, inserting it backward into the socket.

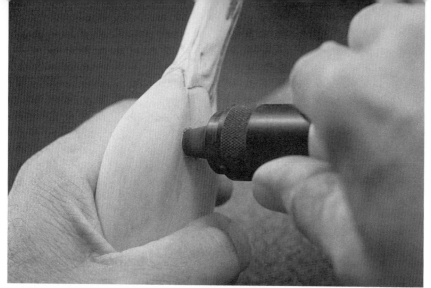

Caution is called for when drilling with a conical bit; you don't want to make the socket too large. Test for fit, then remove just a little more wood until you get a proper fit.

You want a snug fit, says Jim, especially with the first eye. The second eye socket will be made slightly larger; that gives you space to move the eye, aligning it with the first.

The second eye socket is drilled in the same manner as the first, except that it is made slightly larger. Although he carefully located and aligned both eyes before drilling, Jim provides some flexibility in aligning the eyes by making the second socket slightly larger. With both eye sockets drilled, Jim temporarily inserts the right eye and checks for alignment.

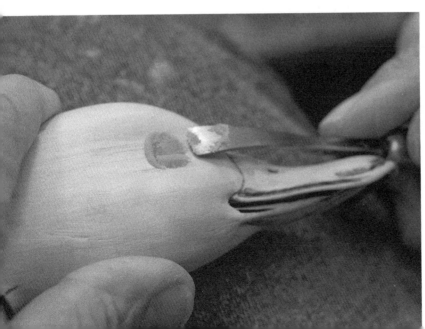

The first step in mounting the eye is to fill the space with wood filler. Immediately press the eye into place while the filler is still soft and pliable. The eye should be pressed into the socket until just a small amount of glass shows when the bird's head is viewed from above.

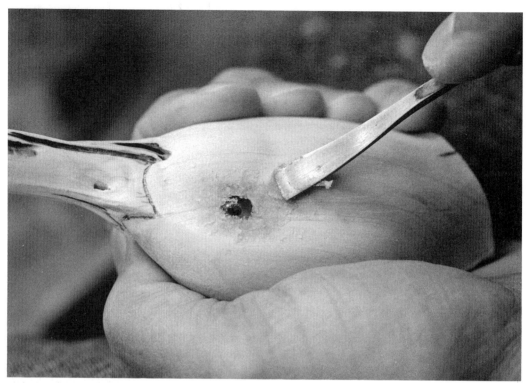

Jim uses a chisel to remove excess putty and
to feather it out. Be careful not to scratch the eye.
Most of the excess putty will be removed with
wood solvent before the material dries.

First, Jim uses a wide sable
brush to clean wood filler from
the eye. It's important, he says,
to use a solvent that is compati-
ble with the wood filler. With
experience, the carver can
virtually eliminate sanding
by using solvents while the
filler material is wet.

A smaller sable brush dipped in solvent is used to open and shape the eye.

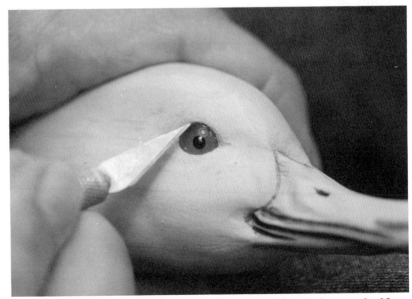

When the filler dries, in approximately one-half hour, Jim uses a small (number 11) X-acto knife to add detail and shape the eye. "I like to do as much as I can with the brush," he says, "but to really dress it up I use that number 11 blade to put in that front corner and add detail."

Jim uses 400-grit sandpaper to clean very carefully around the eye. The goal, he says, is to clean and smooth the eye area. Most of the excess wood filler should be removed with solvent and a brush. The sandpaper is used to smooth the surface rather than to remove filler.

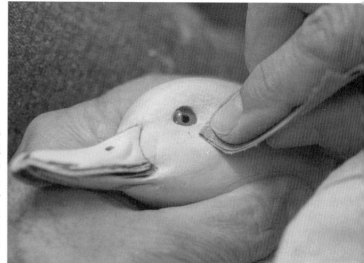

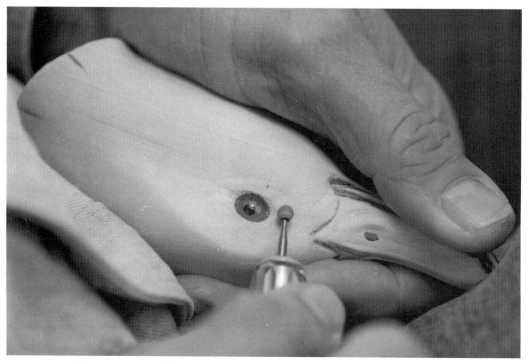

Once the filler is dry, Jim uses a Foredom to clean and shape the area around the eye, creating a smooth transition between the filled area around the glass eye and the wood.

After both eyes are inserted and the area is sanded and finished, Jim goes on to put feather detail in the head. Final work on the eye will come just before painting, when he uses a two-part puttylike resin called plumber's seal to make membranes for the eye, bill, and nostril. In this photograph, Jim has used a burning pen and a stoning tool to create feather detail on the head of the teal. Now he is ready to apply the eye membrane.

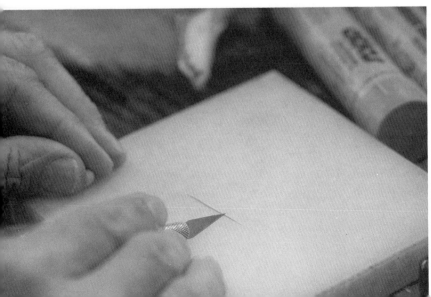

Jim mixes the two parts of the epoxy and uses his finger to roll out a tiny string of putty. Use a clean surface to roll the putty, or it will pick up specks of sandpaper or grit.

Jim makes the string of putty slightly longer than will be needed to go from corner to corner of the eye. The excess will be removed with the X-acto knife. Here he places the string of putty on the lower part of the eye.

A small curved chisel is used to press the putty into place on the eye. It's important at this point not to flatten or distort the shape of the "membrane."

With the putty in place, Jim uses a small sable brush, the same one he used to clean wood filler from the eye, to shape it. He dampens the brush slightly to shape the putty, which is water soluble.

The same procedure is used to create the membrane around the base of the bill and around the nostril. Here, Jim presses the string of putty into place with the curved chisel.

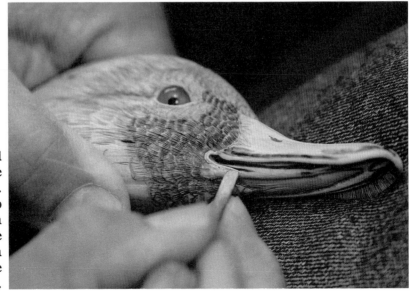

The same tool is used to shape the membrane. A damp sable brush can also be used to smooth and shape the material.

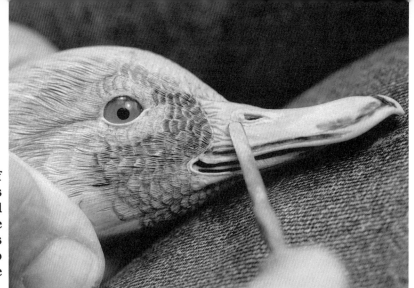

A small ring of
the putty is
placed around
each of the
nostrils and is
pressed into
place with the
curved chisel.

A close-up of the eye area with the putty
membranes in place.

When the putty hardens, the teal is ready for painting. The epoxy membranes add lifelike detail to the bird, which is necessary when carving birds for competition.

The finished head of Jim's cinnamon teal hen . . .

. . . and
the completed
bird.

Jim at work in his Maryland studio, holding the
teal-in-progress. Notice the taxidermy specimen
on the left.

2
Lee and Leo Osborne
Burning the Eye in a Great Blue Heron

Lee and Leo Osborne, who live near the Maine coast in the town of Warren, came to wildfowl art rather indirectly. They left the New England School of Art in 1969, moved to the Maine woods, and lived off the land for several years.

Leo studied illustration in college, but yearned to get into fine art; Lee was a painter. After moving to Maine, Leo worked as a muralist, a sign painter, and a pinstriper for a car dealer. He discovered bird carving in 1980 when attending a local exhibition, invested in some tools, and quickly sold his first two birds to the car dealer. From then on, Lee and Leo have been working professionally as wildfowl artists, and the commissions and awards have been steadily accumulating. Usually, Leo carves and Lee paints, but the two work closely together, sharing ideas and evaluating each other's work.

Leo worked a great deal with large collages when he was at the New England School of Art, and he credits this experience with influencing the bird art he produces today. The Osbornes are perhaps best known for their wall sculptures, simulated blocks of granite on which a bird or two is perched. But the Osbornes' work is indeed eclectic, encompassing everything from realistic songbird carvings to impressionistic wood sculpture. In addition to the wall sculptures, they enjoy working in natural wood, often using burls to sculpt the emerging forms of birds.

In this session, the Osbornes are carving a heron. Both Lee and Leo like to carve a bird from a single piece of wood—no inserts and no glue-ups. They learned from a neighboring carver, Ted Hanks, how to burn in and paint eyes, and they quickly adapted this procedure for their own work. Using the burned-in eye means they can eliminate plastic eye insertions, and because they paint the eye themselves, they can adjust the pupil size to their liking and add highlights.

Lee and Leo in their studio in Warren, Maine. The Osbornes moved to Maine in 1969 and have been carving birds since 1980.

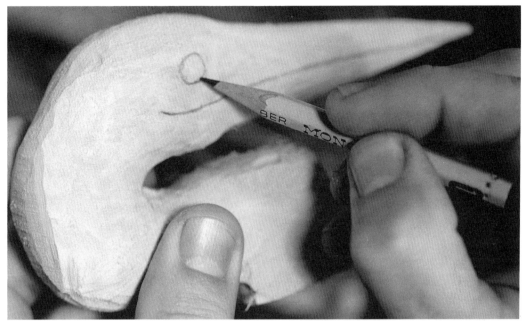

Leo begins the heron by drawing the beak line on both sides of the bird, then locating the eye in relationship to the beak. He does not use a study bird to transfer measurements; instead he studies a wide range of reference materials, mainly photographs, and then "eyeballs" the correct location of the eye.

Once Leo establishes the eye location on one side of the head, he uses that eye to correlate the location of the second eye. "I work on getting the bill line correct, and view it from both sides to make sure that it's accurate and in line."

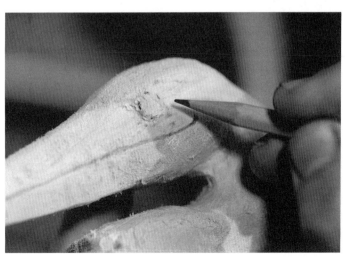

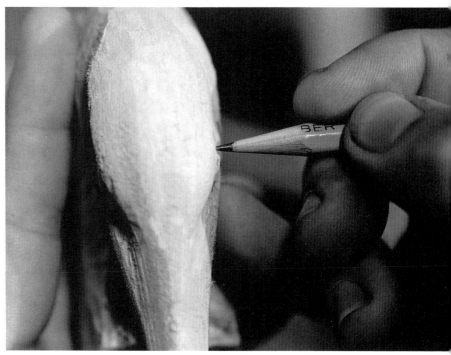

Leo views the head from the front to align the top and bottom of the second eye. Then he views it from the top to determine the back and front of the eye. A pencil mark shows the location.

He views the head from all angles to make sure that the two eyes are in alignment.

It's important when doing the carving to leave enough wood to burn in the eye. The heron has a concave cheek contour, but when carving this be sure to leave plenty of wood at the eye location. It can be removed later, if necessary.

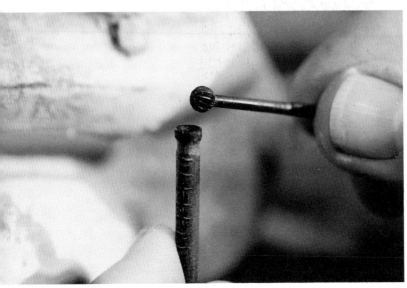

With the beak lines drawn and both eye positions located and aligned, Leo is ready to burn in the eye. He has a collection of steel rods and nails in a variety of sizes, the heads of which have been ground out with a burr like the one shown. This gives them the concave shape that creates the rounded eye.

For the heron, Leo will use a large steel rod, which is heated with a propane torch. Be sure to have all flammables well away from the area when heating the rod, and do the burning in a safe location.

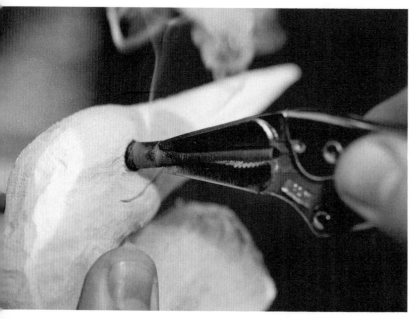

Leo presses the hot rod into the eye location, rotating it to prevent carbon buildup. It's a good idea to practice a few times on a piece of scrap wood before burning the actual eye.

The rod won't retain enough heat to burn the eye in one application. After one burning, the eye is beginning to take shape, but it needs to be deeper.

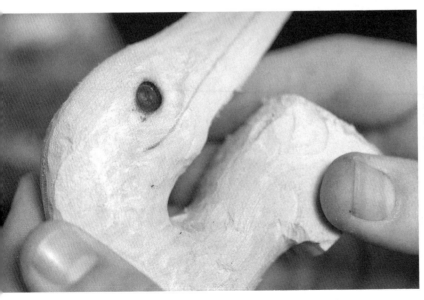

Leo often repeats the procedure several times to arrive at the proper depth. Here, the right eye is nicely shaped, with the top of the eyeball just below the surrounding wood. Leo will later use a rotary cutter to shape and remove some more wood surrounding the eye.

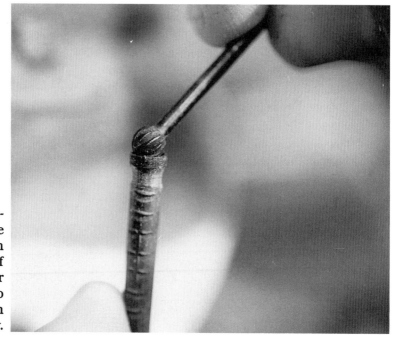

The burning process will create a layer of carbon in the cupped tip of the rod. Use a burr such as this to clean the carbon out periodically.

A wire brush is used to clean carbon and debris from the eye after the burning is completed.

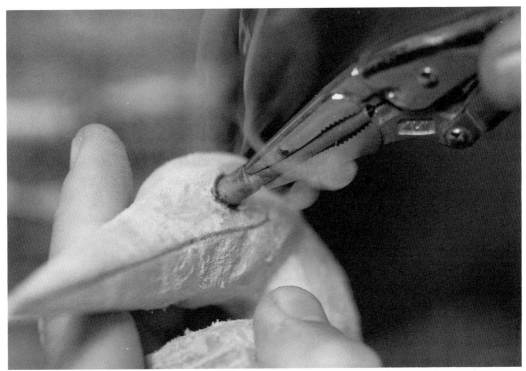

Leo checks eye alignment, and then burns the left eye just as he did the right. The tool is heated and pressed into the wood and is rotated as pressure is applied.

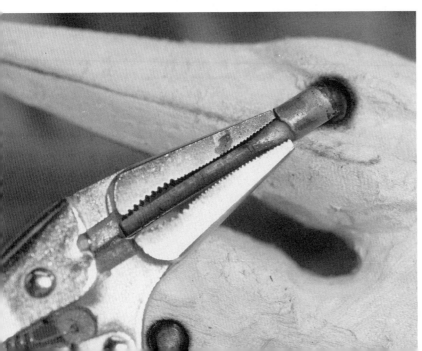

Again, the rod must be cleaned of carbon and reheated several times before the correct depth is achieved.

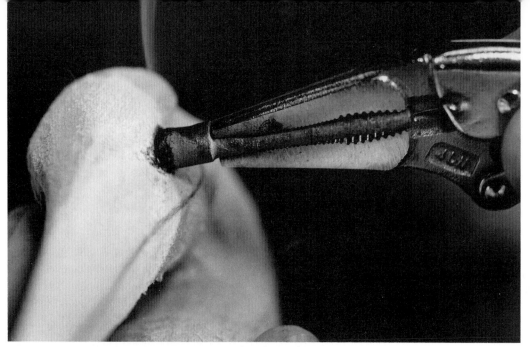

As Leo burns the eye, he checks frequently to
inspect the depth and shape of the eye.

When finished,
the eye will be
nicely rounded,
but a residue
of carbon will
remain.

Leo uses the brush to remove much of the carbon, and a pencil will clean out the deep groove at the edge of the eye. Leo learned the burning technique from Ted Hanks, a former Maryland carver who now lives near the Osbornes on the Maine coast.

Now is the time to inspect the eye area and determine how much wood needs to be removed. Leo uses the wood that remains around the eye to carve the eyelids and brow. He uses a pencil to sketch details and to mark the wood he wants to remove.

A ruby cutter is used to shape the area surrounding the eye. Here Leo is carving the eyelid and brow-line area.

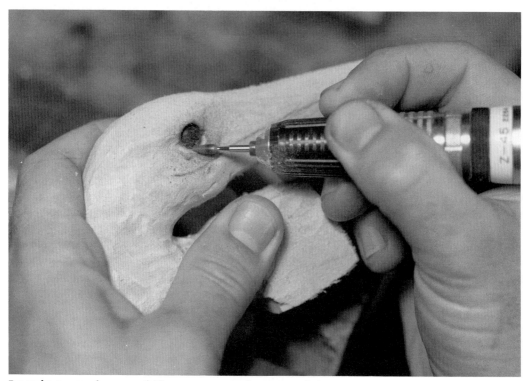

Leaving wood around the eye area when carving the head eliminates having to use fillers or epoxy to add detail.

The area around the left eye is carved in a similar manner. Check the bird from the front and the top to ensure that the same amount of eyeball shows on both sides of the head.

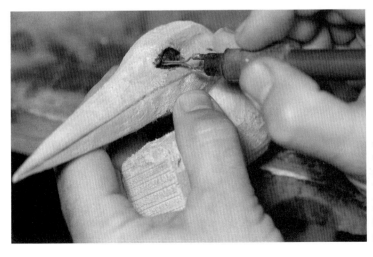

After the area is carved with the ruby cutter, Leo uses a burning tip on low heat to clean up around the eye and add detail.

Leo uses the burning tip mainly to clean up
rough edges left by the ruby cutter. Depending
on the species and your style of carving,
you could use the burning tip to create ridges
along the eyelid and other detail. "You can get as
detailed as you want," says Leo, "depending
upon your personal approach."

Leo doesn't add much detail to the
eye, he just smooths the edges and
rounds contours. When this is
done, the bird is ready for painting.

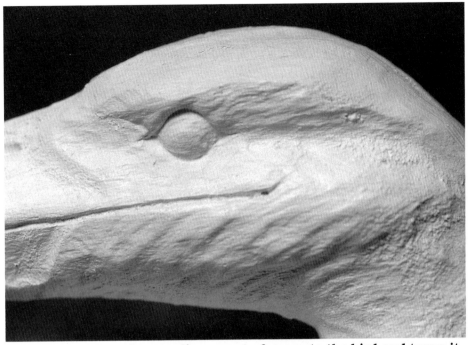

Leo applies a coat of gesso to the bird and turns it over to Lee, who will do the detailed painting.

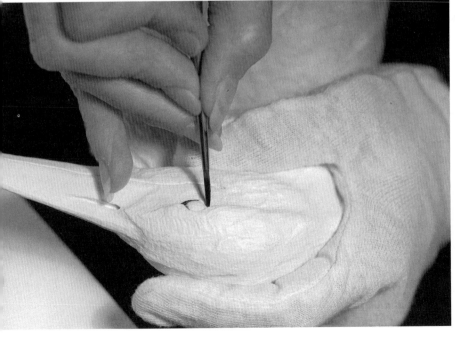

Lee begins by painting the circumference of the eye black. The Osbornes like the burning and painting process because they can control the size of the pupil and add highlights and shadows to the eyes.

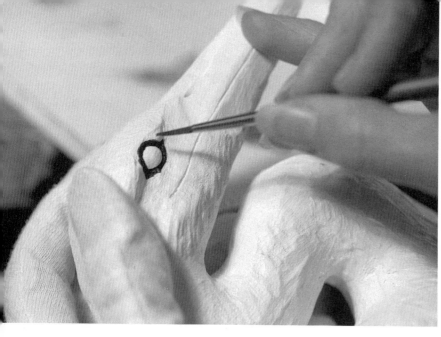

The entire outer
edge of the eyeball is
painted black, with
the paint applied
well onto the eyeball.
Lee wears a cotton
glove on her left
hand to keep the oils
of the skin off the
gessoed surface.

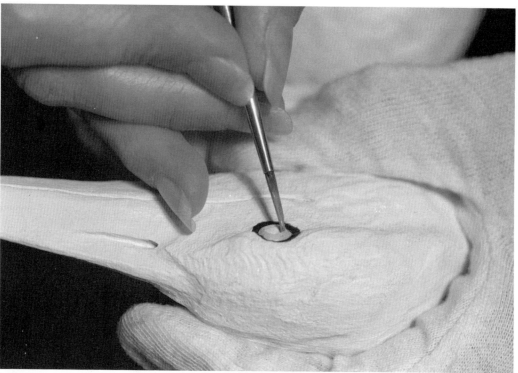

The eyeball is painted yellow, but brown is
added in some areas to create shadow, and white
to add highlights. By changing the tone and
color of the iris, the Osbornes feel they can add
depth and realism to the eye.

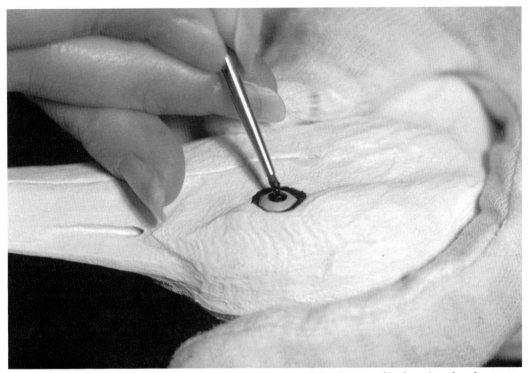

Lee experiments with the pupil size, beginning with a small black pupil and enlarging it as she progresses. Another advantage of the burning and painting process is that if you're not happy with the shadows, highlights, and pupil size, you can always repaint the eye.

And now the eye is finished, with just a few subtle highlights and shadows in the iris. All that remains is the glossy finish that will give it life.

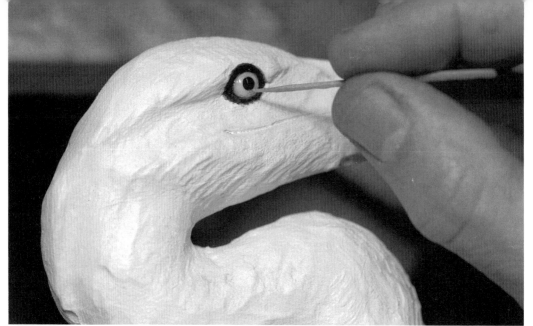

Leo adds gloss by using a toothpick to apply a very thin coat of two-part epoxy. "You just want to cover the eye," he says. "You don't want to put a lot on or it will puddle." Leo applies a dab of epoxy, and then uses another toothpick with a flattened, paperlike edge to spread the material to the outer edges of the eye. Care must be taken not to scratch the paint. You have to work fairly quickly to spread the epoxy before it hardens.

The finished eye. The Osbornes believe a wooden eye is much more realistic than plastic. "Real eyes are not translucent like plastic, they are opaque, with just a glossy film over them," says Leo. "You can create shadows and highlights and control the size of the pupil. And you can do anything with the color you want. If you want to emphasize the effect of sunlight striking a bird, you can create that illusion in the way you paint the eye, adding strong highlights and narrowing the pupil. It's a simple process, but you can accomplish a lot with it."

3

Bob Swain
Carving the Eyes in a Primitive Heron

Duck hunting today might be a shadow of what it once was, but more carvers than ever are making hunting decoys—or decoys in the hunting tradition. Most of these contemporary wooden birds will never float in front of anyone's duck blind. They are instead symbols representing finer times of wildfowl hunting.

Robert Swain, who lives on Virginia's Eastern Shore, doesn't hunt, but he makes shore bird and duck decoys that look like they might have come from Teddy Roosevelt's hunting rig. His carvings are eagerly purchased by hunters who have no intention of taking them into the field.

Bob makes decoys the old-fashioned way—with a saw, a rasp, and a couple of knives. Then, before painting them, he performs the aging ritual. The bird is anointed with a pungent liquid, (dirty paint thinner, says Bob) and then set ablaze.

When the fire subsides—it's a controlled burn— the cedar has lost its fresh-cut gloss and looks as though it has been floating in a swamp for the past hundred years. At this point, Bob is ready to paint.

The painting process involves fire and pigment; the paint is applied, diluted with thinner, and then is set on fire. When the fire is out, the area is cleaned with a bristle brush, and the process is repeated until Bob arrives at the desired color and patina.

In making these instantly aged decoys, Bob is not trying to dupe buyers into thinking they're purchasing something from the 1890s. (He carves his initials into each decoy, and the month and year the bird was carved are stamped onto the lead bottom weight.) It's just that Bob, and those who buy his work, enjoy the fantasy that the bird was carved many years ago. They like the muted colors, the patina, the primitive shape.

In the past ten years or so, the market for wooden decoys has risen even as the waterfowl populations decline. The irony is that while there are fewer birds to hunt than ever before, more hunting-style decoys are being made. The reason, I suspect, is that the decoy is the hunter's tangible link to a time we like to think of as simpler and more fruitful, a time when our planet could still support great populations of waterfowl. In an imperfect world, it is our escape hatch, our ticket to a time that has passed us by.

In this series, Bob Swain carves a heron, which was, and is, a popular confidence decoy that supplements the waterfowler's gunning rig.

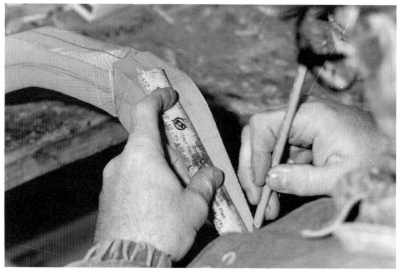

Bob carves his herons from cedar, gluing two pieces of stock together for maximum strength. Because the heron has a long, narrow bill, the grain of the wood should run parallel to the length of the bill. By gluing two pieces of wood together, he avoids having vulnerable cross grain at narrow points, such as the bill and neck. After roughing out the neck and head on the bandsaw, Bob establishes center lines before carving. Here, he uses a straightedge to locate and mark the center line along the top of the bird's head.

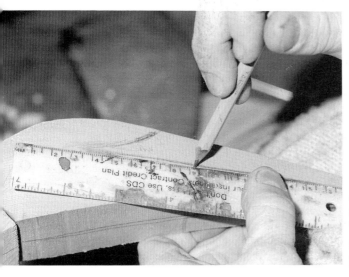

Another line is drawn along the sides of the head and bill. This line serves as a guide during carving; it represents the high points of the head and bill.

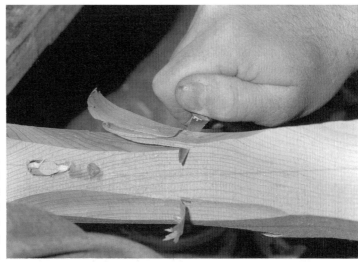

Bob begins by using a knife to round off the neck. At this stage he merely wants to eliminate the sharp edges and to remove excess wood.

The knife is used to clean the area where the two pieces of cedar were joined, smoothing the transition.

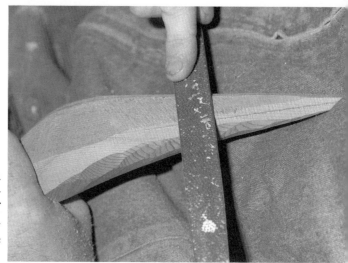

After roughing out the shape with the knife, Bob uses a cabinetmaker's wood rasp to round off the bill and neck. He uses a half-round rasp, which is flat on one side and curved on the other.

The wood rasp removes the flat spots left by the carving knife, rounding off the contours of the carving.

Bob uses the rasp here to smooth the junction of the two pieces of cedar stock. By the time the bird is finished, the joint will not be visible.

Carving a primitive bird such as this heron does not require very many tools. Other than the bandsaw on which the bird was roughed out, Bob uses no other power tools, just knives, a wood rasp, and small chisel.

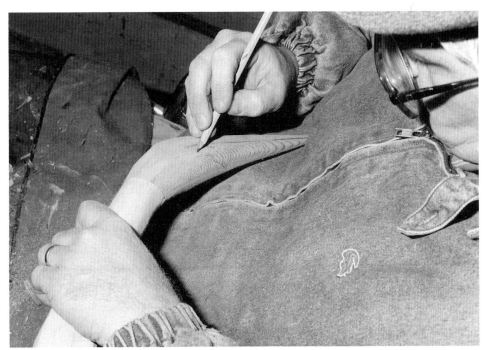

With the heron head rounded into rough shape, Bob uses a pencil to sketch the lines where the bill meets the head. He uses no pattern or reference to locate these lines. He simply sketches them with pencil, and if he's not pleased with the design he will erase the lines and resketch them. Note that the side center line, which represents the high point along the bill, is still visible.

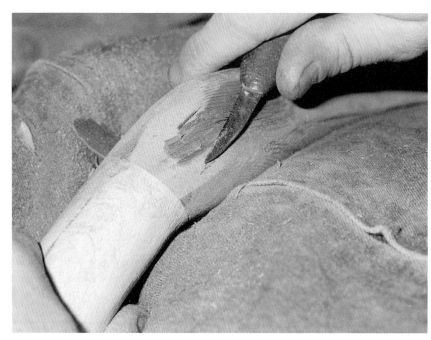

After sketching the head detail, Bob uses a knife to carve the cheek contour where the eye will be located.

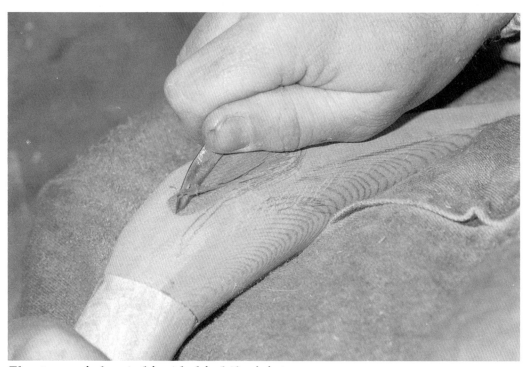

The groove is located just behind the joint of the bill and head, just above the center line marked earlier on the bill.

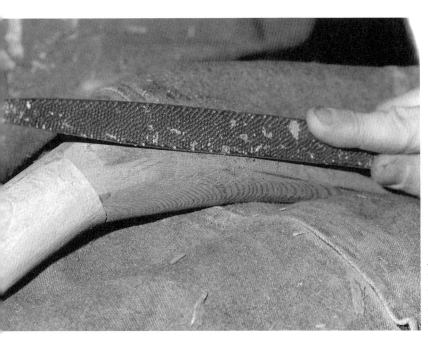

After roughing out
the groove with
the knife, Bob uses the
convex side of the
wood rasp to finish it.

The rasp is used to round out the contours of
the eye groove and to eliminate any flat spots or
gouges left by the knife.

Bob goes over the head and neck of the heron with the rasp one more time to eliminate any flat areas or high spots.

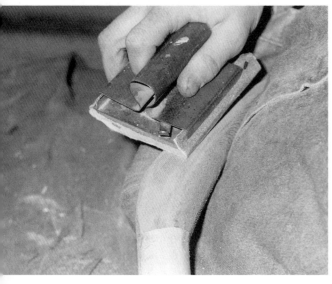

Finally, the eye groove is sanded with medium-grit paper, and Bob is ready to sketch and carve the eye.

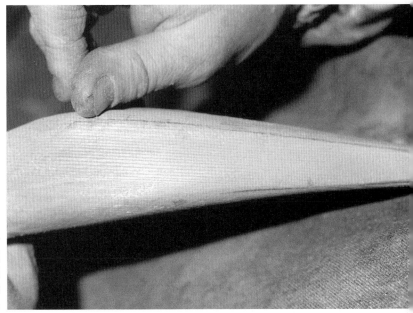

Note that the center line he established before carving is still visible along the side of the head.

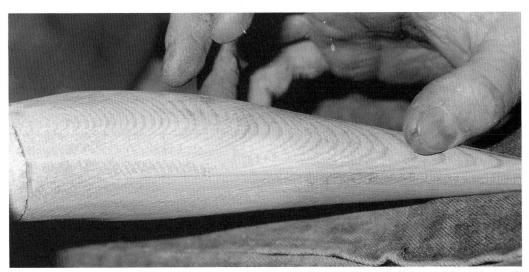

The center line also remains visible on the top and bottom of the head. These lines establish high points and are a critical reference in establishing the shape of the head.

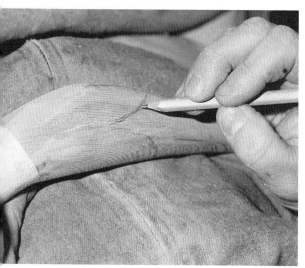

The location of these lines is established by eye. Bob will sketch and erase the lines several times until he is happy with the look of the bird. Once the head–bill lines are established, Bob uses a knife to relieve the bill.

Bob uses a pencil to again sketch the joint between bill and head and the eye location.

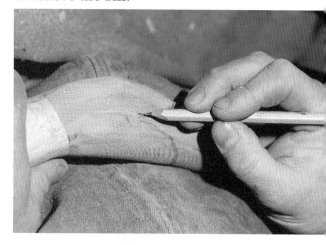

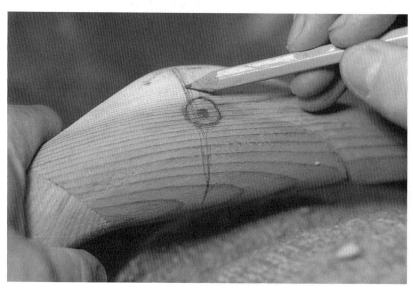

Another center line is drawn vertically along the head of the heron. The eye should be located along the carved eye groove and slightly forward of the center line.

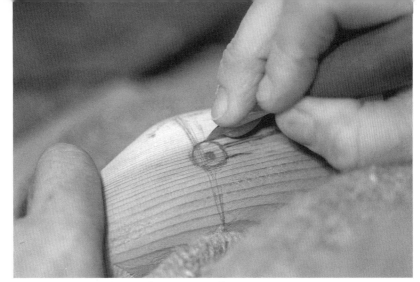

When Bob is happy with the eye placement, he begins carving the eye with a small knife, tracing the outline of the eye with the knife.

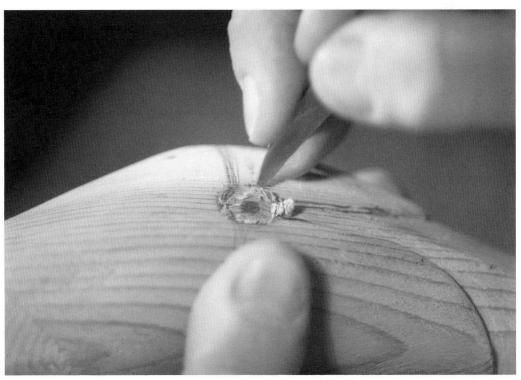

The cut should be made deeper along the outside circumference of the eye, giving the eye its convex shape. The pupil Bob sketched onto the eye is left as a high point.

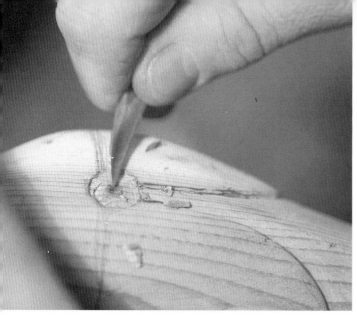

Bob uses the small knife to make a shallow cut around the pupil. The center of the pupil will remain high, and the deeper cut at the edges of the eye will give it roundness.

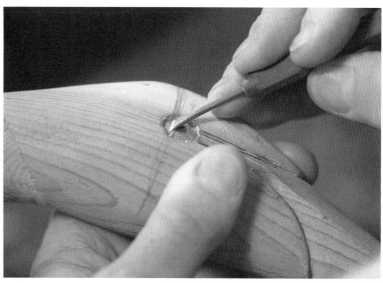

Once the knife cuts are made, Bob uses a tiny chisel to remove wood, beginning at the shallow cut near the pupil, moving to the deeper cuts at the outer margin of the eye.

The carved eye and the relieved bill detail look like this. Note how the lines of the bill join the eye to create a pleasing design.

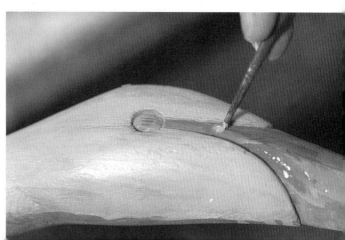

With the carving completed, Bob distresses the wood by burning. He applies a solution of "dirty thinner" to the head and bill, and ignites it with a match. Extreme care should be taken if you attempt to do this. Be sure that all flammables are out of the area, and do the burn in a safe area, where the flames can set nothing else on fire.

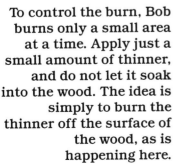

To control the burn, Bob burns only a small area at a time. Apply just a small amount of thinner, and do not let it soak into the wood. The idea is simply to burn the thinner off the surface of the wood, as is happening here.

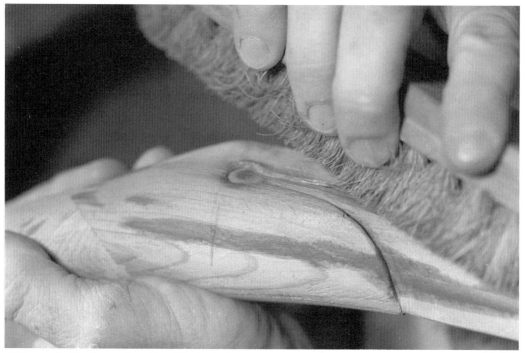

After briefly burning the bird, Bob uses a
heavy scrub brush to buff it. Sometimes he will
repeat the burn–buff procedure several times
until he achieves the desired patina.

After two or three
burnings, the wood
is no longer white
and fresh looking. It
appears nicely aged,
providing a good
base for painting.

Bob begins by applying a coat of white oil-base paint to the head of the heron. He uses Mohawk brand Japan paint, which dries extremely fast.

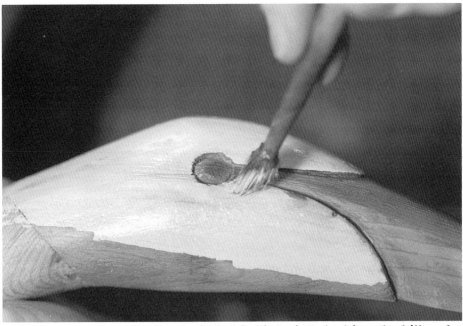

The head of the bird is painted white; the bill and eye will remain unpainted for now.

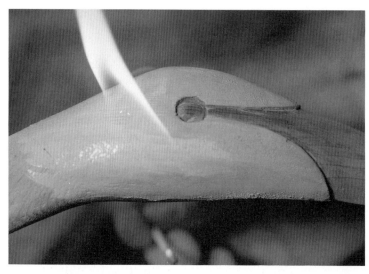

While the paint is still wet, Bob again sets the head on fire. Instead of using thinner this time, Bob sets fire directly to the paint.

When the fire burns out, he uses the scrub brush to buff what remains of the coat of white. He will repeat the process until he achieves a pleasing patina. "Some people use burning only as an accent," he says, "but I use it as a major painting technique."

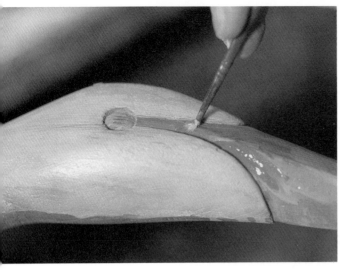

The bill is painted with a combination of white and raw sienna. He mixes the two colors on a palette until he arrives at a basic yellow-orange bill color, then he applies more raw sienna to the mixture while painting the bill. "That way you don't get a constant color; it becomes slightly mottled."

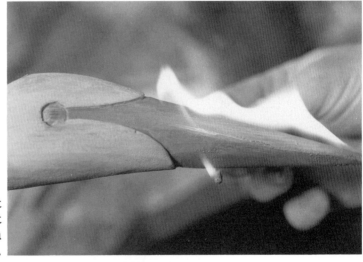

Again, the bill is set on fire after the paint is applied, and then is brushed.

Several applications may be necessary to achieve the correct "aged" look. Here the pigment blisters under the heat, but the surface paint will be buffed off when the fire subsides.

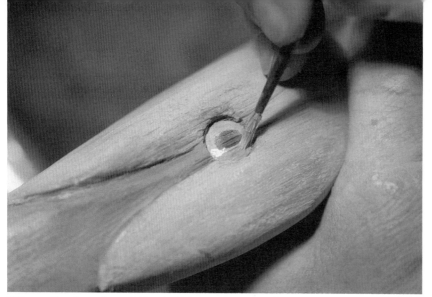

When the head and the bill have been painted,
Bob turns to the eyes, first applying a coat of raw
sienna and white to the iris.

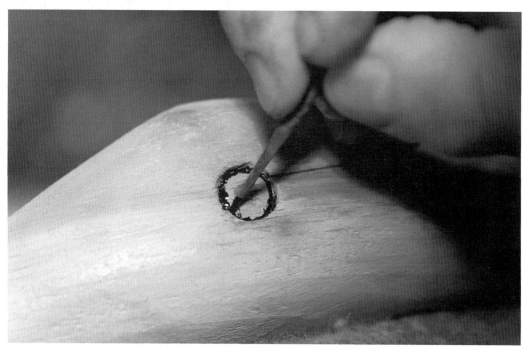

Then a black ring is painted around the circumference of the eye. The paint will again be burned
and buffed, feathering one color into another, so
neatness is not critical at this stage.

Black is also applied to the pupil of the bird's eye.

Small highlights can be painted in if desired.

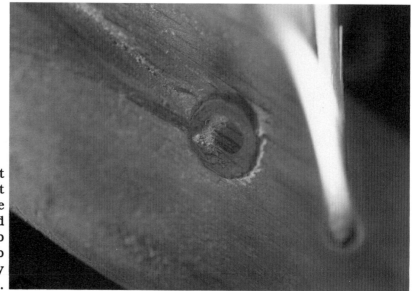

Again the wet paint is set on fire, and the eye is buffed with the scrub brush until Bob is happy with the patina.

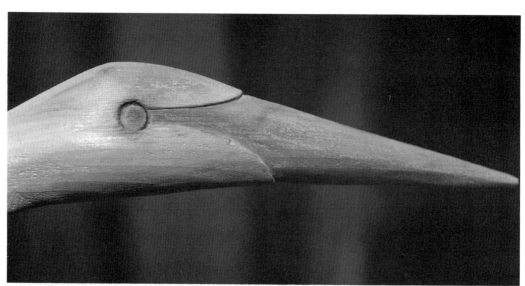

The finished heron head has a simple, sleek design that goes well with the aged look of the paint. The carving is modern, yet it borrows much from the look of the past.

4

Pete Peterson
Inserting a Canvasback Eye

"Hurricane" Pete Peterson, so named because of his ability to produce high-quality decoys faster than a hundred-knot breeze, keeps a low profile these days. The only show he enters is the Easton Wildfowl Festival, and he's not looking for more orders. Pete doesn't believe in competitions, and he has tired of going to all the shows and replying to all the standard questions: How long does it take? What kind of wood? How much do you want for it?

Pete seems most comfortable in his cluttered carving shop on Virginia's Eastern Shore. There's a picture on the wall of one of Pete's heroes, Nathan Cobb, Jr., who carved decoys a century ago on an island just a few miles from Pete's shop. (Pete's house once belonged to the Cobb family.) There's an old chopping block, a small wood stove, and a shaving horse that looks as though it might have been used by old Nathan himself. There are paints, pictures, and dozens of decoys in various stages of dress. The room is ankle deep in white cedar shavings and has a heady aroma you'd like to bag and sell. It's a room that tickles the senses. You don't live in it—you wear it.

Pete carves traditional decoys, but with his own brand and in his own style. He likes traditional tools: the drawknife, shaving horse, hatchet, knife. The bandsaw is in a separate shop, and the only concessions to the twentieth century in Pete's studio are an electric light, a radio tuned to country music, and an electric drill with one of P. C. English's special bits for inserting eyes. Pete likes the bit because it provides a pistonlike fit for the glass eye, which means he can mount the eye without using wood filler, which is messy and time-consuming. He has several bits, each a different size for different eyes.

Pete's no-filler approach to eye insertion differs from that of most carvers, and his carving technique differs in other respects as well. He doesn't locate the eyes until the head is mounted on the body because he wants to be able to see the entire bird when he decides where the eye will be placed.

While most carvers insert the eye before mounting the head onto the body, Pete doesn't actually insert the eye until the carving is almost completed. The head is mounted, the eye location is determined, the socket is drilled, the bird is painted, and then finally the eye goes in. This procedure is cleaner, quicker, and less messy than attempting to paint around a mounted eye.

In addition to making traditional decoys, Pete carves folk art items such as fish. In this session, Pete demonstrates how he locates and inserts an eye in a canvasback, then he shows a quick and easy method of carving eyes using the casings of rifle cartridges.

Visiting Pete's carving shop is like stepping back in time a century or so. He prefers to carve the old-fashioned way, with traditional tools and techniques. Although he roughs out his juniper blanks on the bandsaw, the remainder of the work is done with hand tools, such as a hatchet.

One of Pete's most important tools is this shaving horse, an ancient design that has been used over the years by many types of craftsmen. Pete finds it ideal for holding a decoy body while he carves the body with a drawknife.

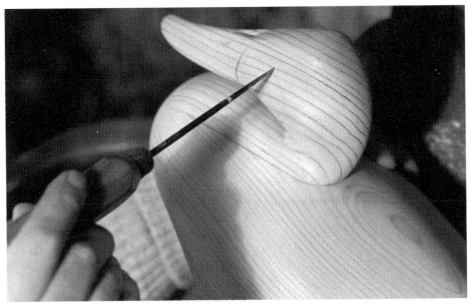

Pete's procedure for locating and inserting eyes differs from that of many carvers. He believes in mounting the head on the body before inserting the eye because he can see the entire bird. "I like to see the whole bird at one time when I determine the location of the eye," says Pete. "I don't like having the head loose."

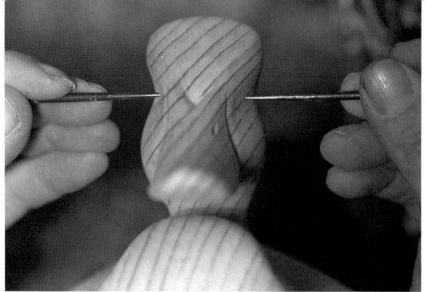

Pete uses two ice picks, or awls, to determine the
eye position. He doesn't measure from a study bird
or use any other direct reference, although he
does keep photographs of various species in his
studio. The eye of a canvasback is located along a
plane established by the line of the bill, as Pete
points out in a photograph. It's important that the
eyes be symmetrical and in alignment. Pete uses
two ice picks here because with their long shafts
he can easily check alignment by moving the
shafts until they are parallel with each other.

Alignment should be checked
from the top of the head and
from the front. Having one
eye higher than the other, or
farther forward, can quickly
ruin the appearance of an
otherwise well-made decoy.
Also, Pete cautions, don't use
eyes that are too large for the
bird. For this canvasback,
Pete will use 7mm glass eyes.

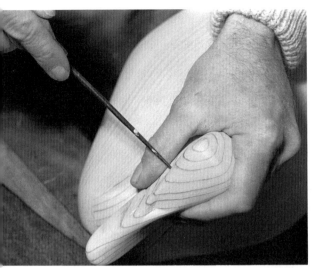

Once both eye locations are aligned, Pete uses the ice pick to mark the location. The point of the ice pick is pressed into the wood, creating a pilot hole for his drill bit.

Pete uses a bit made especially for drilling eye sockets. This bit is designed for inserting 7mm eyes, and it has a small pilot bit to ensure that the larger bit doesn't wander off target. The cutting edge of the main bit is designed to prevent tearing the wood, thus providing a clean cut.

Because of the irregular surface of the head, you can't use a stop on the bit to control the depth of the cut. If you purchase a bit such as this, practice with it on scrap wood to get a feel for the cutting speed. After drilling a few holes and test fitting some glass eyes, you'll soon learn how deep to make your sockets.

Pete drills for a few seconds, then removes the bit to check the depth. At this point, the socket is ready for eye insertion. Unlike many carvers, Pete does not use wood filler as a medium for mounting the eye. If you use filler, you'll want to make the socket slightly deeper. The advantage of this tool, however, is that the cut can be made precisely enough that filler is not required. No matter what technique you use, practice on scrap wood before attempting the procedure on the real thing.

With the right eye socket of the canvasback completed, Pete drills the socket on the left side, again using the dimple left by the ice pick as a pilot hole. The socket hole is drilled to exactly the same depth as the first socket.

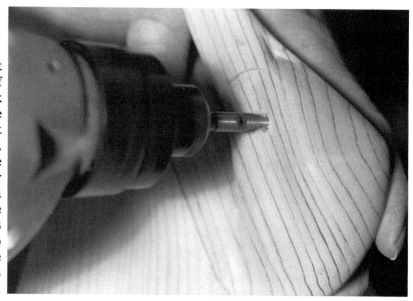

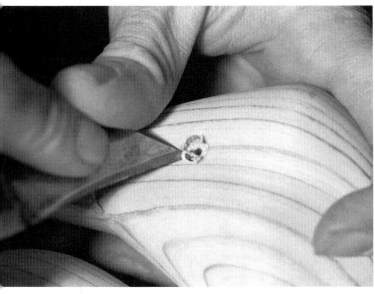

With both eye sockets drilled, Pete uses a sharp knife to slightly chamfer the circumference of the eye socket. This creates a more natural transition between the eye and the surrounding wood, simulating the membrane of a live bird.

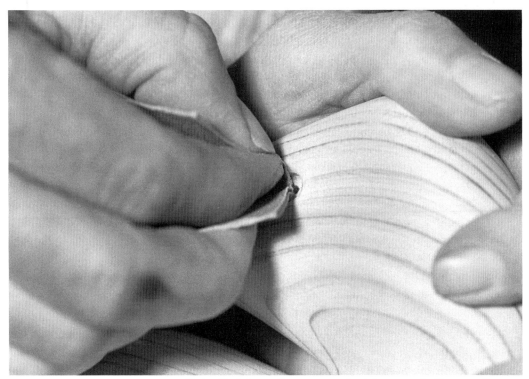

Pete finishes the eye socket by carefully sanding the circumference with fine sandpaper.

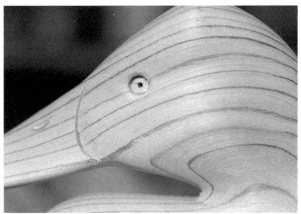

And now, the eye is ready for insertion. Notice how Pete chamfered and softened the area surrounding the eye. The small hole left by the pilot bit will take the wire shaft of the glass eye.

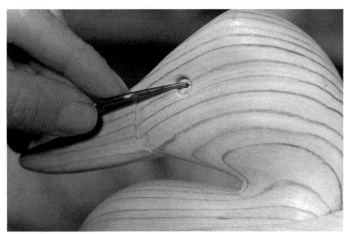

Notice that the line of the bill is on an axis with the eye as the center point. Pete says that studying taxidermy is a good way to learn eye location and the relationship of the eye and bill. "If you study the skull of a bird, you'll quickly see the relationship of the eye socket and the bill," says Pete. "I haven't done taxidermy for a long time, but when I locate the eye, I still use that mental picture of the skull."

The glass eye is slightly larger than the eye socket, ensuring a tight fit. Most of the time, Pete will paint the bird before inserting the eye because it makes it easier to paint around the eye. For demonstration purposes, he will insert the eye in the canvasback at this point.

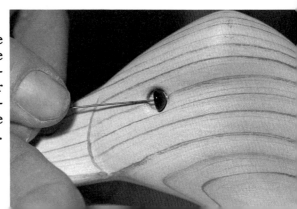

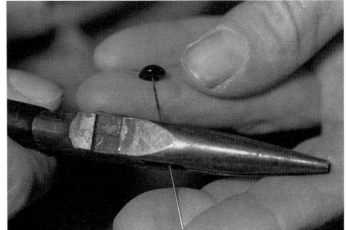

Pete uses glass eyes with a wire mounting shaft, leaving about five-eighths of an inch of wire on the eye. This shaft will be pressed into the hole left by the pilot bit.

Because the fit is very tight, it will take some force to press the eye into place. Pete uses the end of a broom handle, which is soft enough that it will not scratch the surface of the eye. Put pressure directly on the center of the eye and be sure that the eye goes in squarely. If it goes in at an angle it will not seat correctly and will have to be removed. To remove the eye, Pete uses a nail set and a hammer to shatter it, then extracts the remains with needle-nose pliers. The fit is so tight that the eye cannot be removed any other way without damaging the wood surrounding it, Pete says.

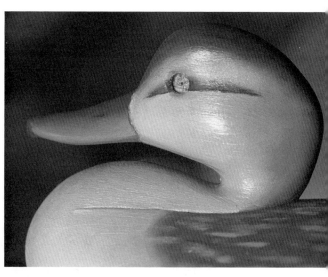

This eye-insertion procedure allows Pete to paint the bird without having to worry about getting paint on the eye and having to scrape it off, possibly scratching the eye in the process. Normally, inserting the eye is one of the final steps in the carving process. This teal, for example, has been painted, and now needs only to have the glass eye pressed into place.

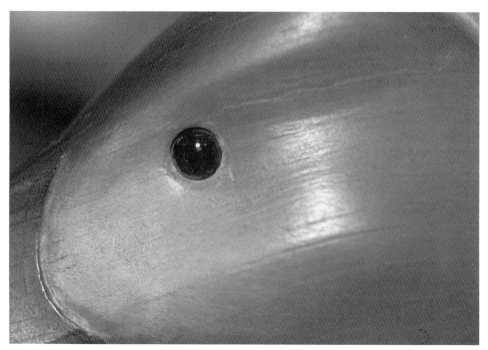

The canvasback hen with the inserted eye. Pete's technique of inserting the eye without using filler as a mounting medium speeds up the carving process, and makes it cleaner and neater. The only caveat is that the eye socket must provide a precise fit. The drill bits used by Pete are designed for this purpose. They are available from carving supply dealers. Pete ordered his from the P. C. English Company.

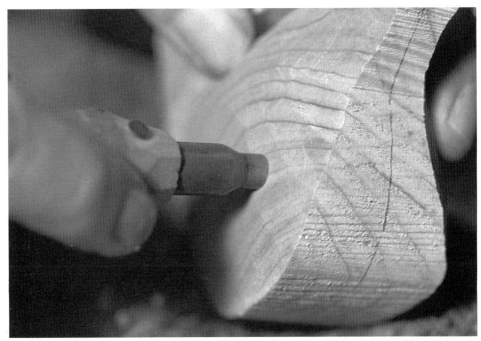

In addition to duck decoys, Pete carves shore birds and folk art fish, and sometimes he carves eyes rather than inserting lifelike glass ones. For this procedure, Pete has a collection of different caliber rifle cartridges whose edges have been sharpened. Depending on the size of eye needed, Pete selects a cartridge casing, presses it into the head, and instantly creates the outline of an eye.

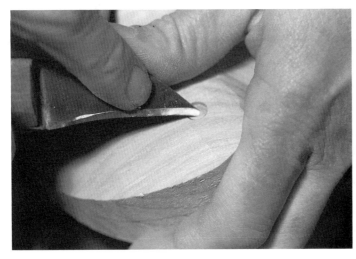

After creating the outline of the eye, Pete uses a sharp knife to carve the eyeball, leaving a high spot in the middle of the eye and tapering it down to the circumference of the eye.

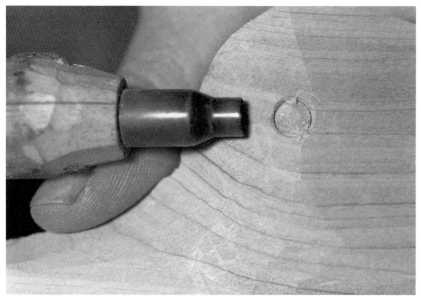

This procedure makes carving eyes quick and easy. It takes Pete only a few seconds to carve a nice folk-art eye. To make the shell casings easier to use, Pete mounts them in wooden rods, drilling a recess into the end of the rod that the shell casing will fit snugly into.

A carved fish eye provides a nice folk-art touch.

5

Grayson Chesser
Inserting the Eyes in a Wood Duck Decoy

Grayson Chesser became involved in decoy carving through a childhood passion for waterfowl hunting, and now, at forty-three, the two pursuits are so closely interwoven they are impossible to separate. Grayson enjoys hunting because it gives him a chance to prove the quality of his decoys in the field. And he enjoys decoy making because it is a logical extension of hunting.

At some point in the early part of this century, most decoy carvers began making birds with the buyer in mind, crafting a carving that would appeal to humans rather than birds. Grayson belongs to the earlier generation; although his decoys are more often purchased by collectors than hunters, he still carves for the eye of the bird, not the eye of the buyer. While many contemporary carvers tend to streamline their decoys, making them more pleasing to the human eye, Grayson's decoys are often slightly oversize, just what you'd need for hunting.

His approach to eye insertion is traditional. He establishes the location visually, drawing a black dot with a pencil. When he is satisfied with the location, he draws a circle around the dot, which represents the circumference of the eye. He uses a knife to cut out the eye socket, and then he fills the hole with wood filler before inserting the eye. A wire shaft is left attached to the eye, and this is pressed into the wood at the base of the socket, ensuring a tight fit. When the eye is seated, Grayson wipes away excess filler, then sands the area when the filler dries.

In this session, Grayson is making a gunning-style wood duck. He uses an 8mm black glass eye whether he's making a drake or a hen.

Grayson does not use measurements or cast reference birds to locate the eyes. Instead, he does it visually, drawing a black dot at what he believes is the proper position. With species he does not carve often, he will sometimes use a photograph as a reference. He draws black dots on both sides of the head, and checks from the front and top to make sure the alignment is correct.

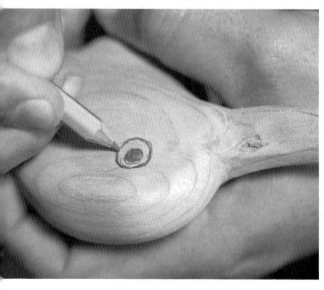

Grayson then draws around the dot a circle that is slightly larger than the circumference of the eye. Grayson will use 8mm glass eyes for the wood duck, but the hole will be slightly larger to accommodate wood filler in which the eye will be mounted.

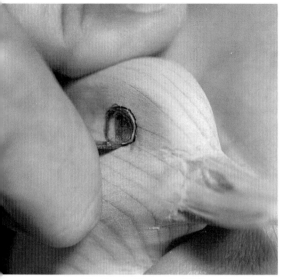

Rather than drilling the hole, Grayson uses a sharp knife with a small blade to cut around the circumference of the eye.

As the cut is made, it's important not to chip away any wood around the eye or to let the knife blade wander off course. A sharp knife is essential.

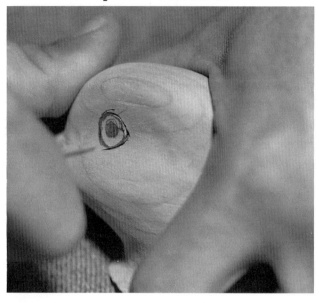

The cut should be slightly deeper than the thickness of the glass eye. Wood filler will form a backing for the eye and cement it in place.

When the cut is completed, it will look like this.
Both eyes should be cut at this point.

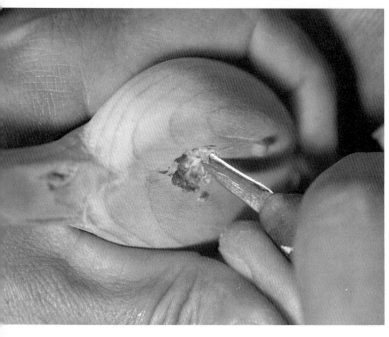

With the outer edge of
the eye cut, Grayson uses
the knife to chip out the
center part of the eye.

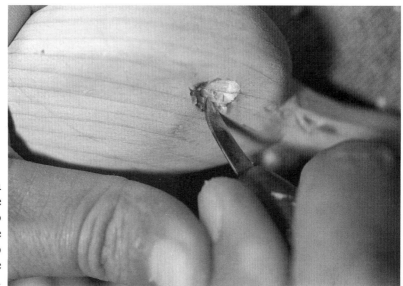

This is done on both sides of the head. Check to be sure the hole is deep enough to accommodate the glass eye.

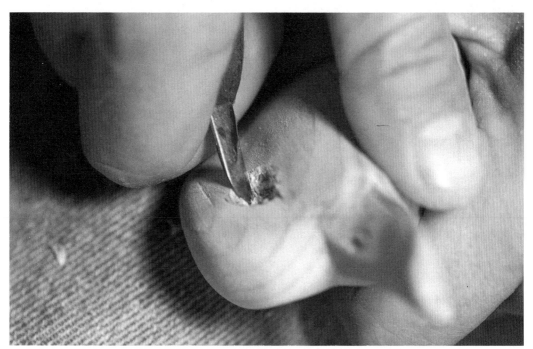

Before mounting the eye, Grayson presses the knife blade into the eye socket to soften the wood. The eye has a metal mounting stem, which will be pressed into the wood like a tack.

The glass eyes Grayson uses have long metal stems, which he cuts with wire cutters.

For most applications, Grayson leaves about one-quarter of an inch of metal stem attached to the eye.

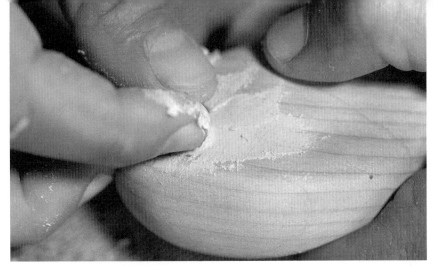

The next step is to fill the eye socket with wood filler. There are a number of suitable brands. Grayson uses Fam-O-Wood here. Plastic Wood is also a popular brand.

It's important to fill the eye socket completely with the filler, leaving no air holes or cavities. Be generous with the filler; excess will be scraped away. Because the filler dries rapidly, do only one eye at a time.

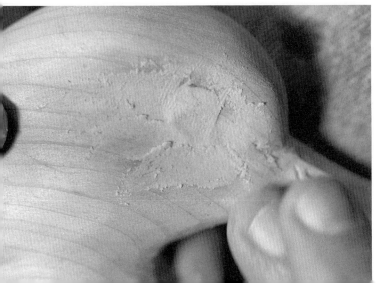

Grayson covers a large area with the filler, which not only will hold the eye in place, but will also create an eyelid and fill in any knife marks or scratches around the eye socket.

73

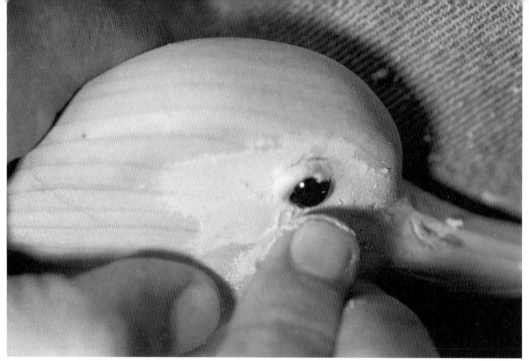

While the filler is still moist and pliable,
Grayson presses the glass eye into position. It
should fit fairly tightly in the socket,
pressing into the wood filler.

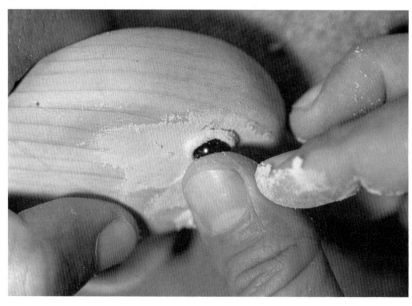

Because of the
metal stem,
some force
must be used to
press the eye
all the way into
place. Grayson
uses his thumb,
pressing the eye
in like a tack.
Using the knife
point to soften
the wood (page 71,
bottom) makes it
easier to press
the eye into
position.

Press the eye in until you can feel it rest against the back of the socket. The mounting stem will help keep the eye in place, and the wood filler will hold it in position permanently when it dries.

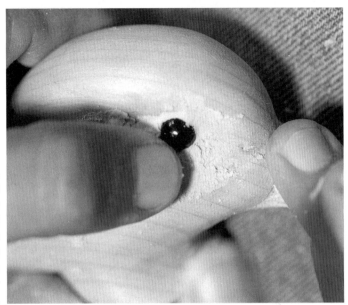

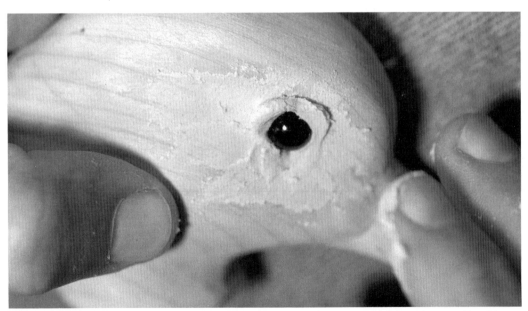

When the glass eye is pressed into the cavity, it will force out excess filler. You can wipe this away with your finger while the putty is still pliable. As much as possible, try to keep filler off the surface of the eye.

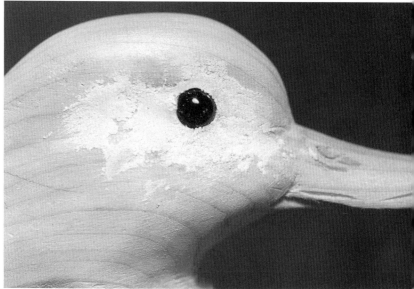

Grayson has mounted the right eye, and the wood filler is beginning to dry. As it dries, he will turn the head over and use the same procedure in mounting the left eye.

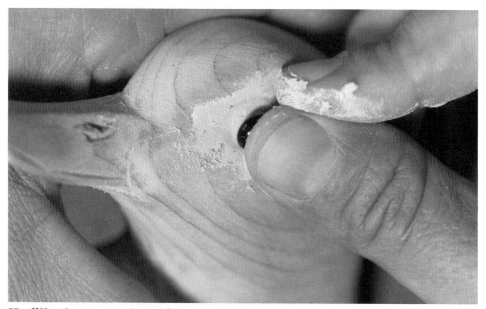

He fills the eye socket with wood filler, then presses the glass eye into place. Some carvers like to make the second eye socket slightly larger than the first because it gives them the flexibility to change the position of the eye slightly, correcting any alignment problems.

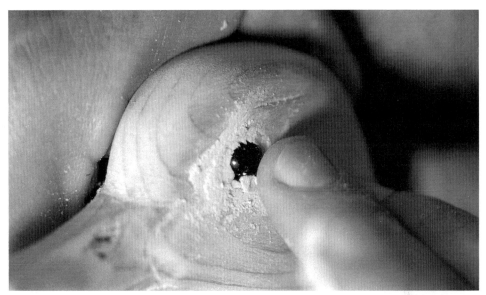

Again, Grayson uses a generous amount of filler, which will fill in around the eye and create the illusion of an eye membrane.

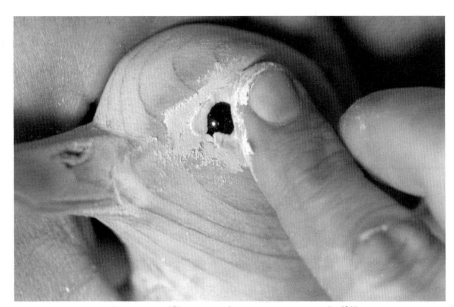

Grayson likes to clean up as much filler as possible while it is still moist. The more you have to sand and scrape around the eye, the more likely you are to scratch the surface.

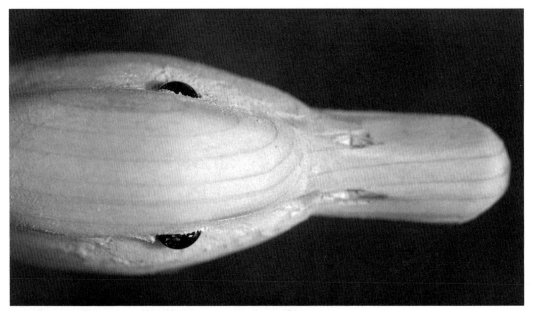

While the filler is still pliable, check for alignment from the top. An equal amount of eye should show on each side. Some correction can be made at this stage, but it's best to trial fit the eyes before planting them in wood filler.

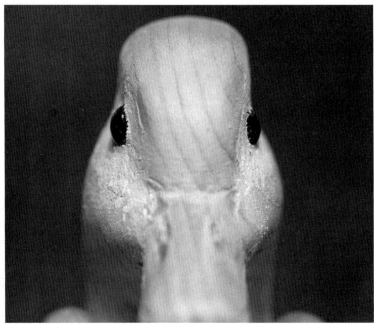

Now check the alignment from the front. Note how the wood filler creates the illusion of an eyelid, or membrane, around the eye.

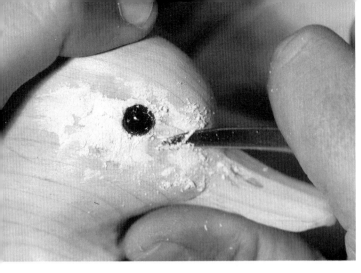

Grayson uses a knife with a long blade to scrape away excess wood filler. The long blade makes it less likely he will scratch or cut the surface of the wood.

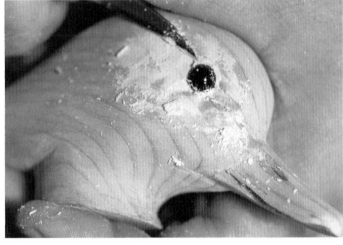

When working near the glass eye, Grayson uses extreme care. The eye is very fragile and a slight scratch will diminish the lifelike appearance of the bird.

As shown here, the wood filler not only acts as a mounting medium for the eye, but it fills in any scratches or depressions around the eye.

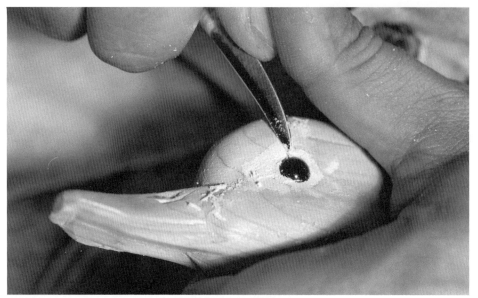

When the filler around the left eye is dry,
Grayson repeats the procedure on that side, again
taking care not to scratch the glass eye.

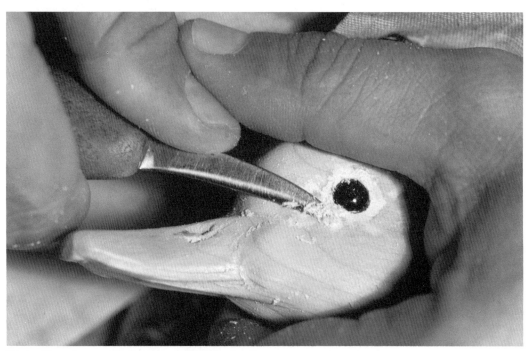

Note the size and shape of the blade Grayson
uses for the cleanup. A smaller blade or a chisel
could gouge the surface of the wood.

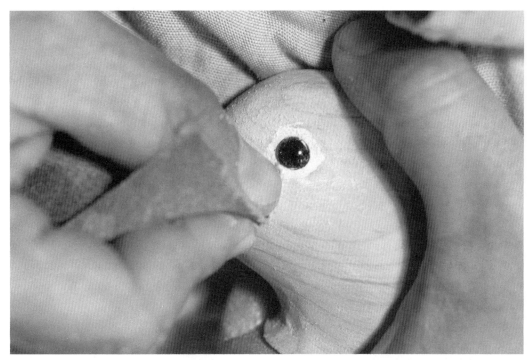

With most of the filler removed by the blade, Grayson then uses very fine sandpaper to clean the area.

The area immediately surrounding the eyeball should be sanded lightly, but be very careful not to let the abrasive material come in contact with the surface of the eye.

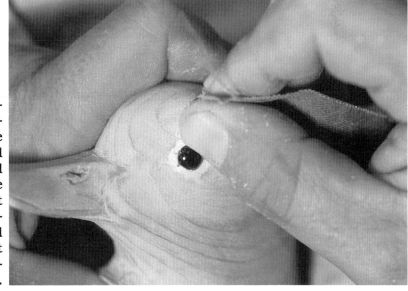

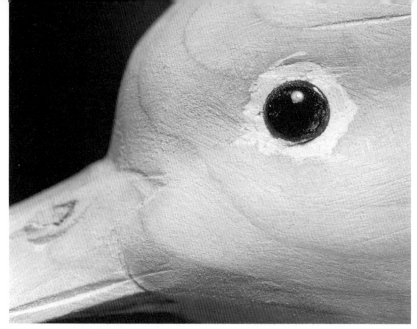

In this close-up of the left eye, you can see how the filler anchors the eye and also creates something of an eyelid.

On the right side, the material also fills in some small depressions and scratches. At this point, the wood duck head is ready to be mounted to the body and then painted.

About the Author

Curtis Badger has written widely about wildfowl art, wildfowl hunting, and conservation issues in general. His articles have appeared in many national and regional magazines, and he serves as editor of *Wildfowl Art Journal,* which is published by the Ward Foundation. He is currently working with carver Jim Sprankle on a book on wildfowl painting techniques, and he is writing a book about growing up on the Virginia coast. He lives in Onley, Virginia.

Other Books of Interest to Bird Carvers

Bird Carving Basics: Feet
A wide variety of techniques for creating all kinds of wildfowl feet.
by Curtis J. Badger

How to Carve Wildfowl
The masterful techniques of nine international blue-ribbon winners.
By Roger Schroeder

How to Carve Wildfowl Book 2
Features eight more master carvers and the tools, paints, woods, and techniques they use
for their best-in-show carvings.
By Roger Schroeder

Waterfowl Carving with J. D. Sprankle
A fully illustrated reference to carving and painting 25 decorative ducks.
by Roger Schroeder and James D. Sprankle

Making Decoys the Century-Old Way
Detailed, step-by-step instructions on hand-making the simple yet functional working
decoys of yesteryear.
By Grayson Chesser and Curtis J. Badger

How to Paint Songbirds
How to Paint Shorebirds
How to Paint Owls
How to Paint Gamebirds
Watercolor, gouache, and acrylic techniques, beautiful color sequences, and detailed paint-
ing instructions show how to add life to bird paintings on any surface.
by David Mohrhardt

John Scheeler, Bird Carver
A tribute to the bird-carving world's master of masters, John Scheeler.
by Roger Schroeder

Carving Miniature Wildfowl with Robert Guge
Scale drawings, step-by-step photographs and painting keys demonstrate the techniques
that make Guge's miniatures the best in the world.
by Roger Schroeder and Robert Guge

Songbird Carving with Ernest Muehlmatt
Muehlmatt shares his expertise on painting, washes, feather flicking, and burning, plus
insights on composition, design, proportion, and balance.
by Roger Schroeder and Ernest Muehlmatt

For complete ordering information, write:
Stackpole Books
P.O. Box 1831
Harrisburg, PA 17105
or call 1-800-READ-NOW